….Taking …………
… ……………………
Flight, ………………
………………………………………**Following Through**.
………………
……………………………………………………**……..Letting**
….
……………………………………………… ……….
… ….. ………...... ……………………………….**go**
………………………………… ………….

Metanoia; ………………..
The journey of changing one's heart, mind, self, or way of life.

…………………………………………
………….. ……………. ……………………………………………………………………
Being still. …………………………………………..
……………………………………….
………………………………………………

Joshua Purnell

Metanoia

Copyright © 2024 Joshua Purnell

All rights reserved. No part of this publication may be reproduced, distributed, or transmitted in any form or by any means, including photocopying, recording, or other electronic or mechanical methods, without the prior written permission of the publisher, except in the case of brief quotations embodied in critical reviews and certain other noncommercial uses permitted by copyright law.

Send permission requests to the following address:
620 W 28th St, Norfolk, VA 23508, USA
Email: leaveit2joshua@gmail.com

Cover photography by Joshua Purnell.
Published by Joshua Purnell.
ISBN: 9798320161105
Printed in The United States of America

To whoever is seeking truth,
to whoever is trying to heal,
to striving to grow,
to LOVE,
to Bryan Stage,
our Local Legend.

Foreword

 I first met Joshua entering our Arts and Culture exchange at the Columbus, Mississippi public library as he juggled a load of ukuleles and beautiful canvases of art, radiating curiosity and friendliness. Throughout the afternoon, he shared songs he'd written, playing and singing along gently with a friend, and spread out the gorgeous paintings of skies, which were only a fraction of his collection of both art and song. The combination of his gentle, energetic presence and the beauty and skill of his unassuming art made it clear there is so much to learn from Joshua Purnell.

 After a few interactions we noticed we both love a very free hand with ideas and form in writing, and he let me read a manuscript he'd been working on for a while, an early version of Metanoia. Reading through this script was a chance to sit at the mountaintop and in the concert hall at the same time. He deftly leaps from the immediacy of the now-- a sore hip while sitting on the riverbank and watching a bird fly low over the water-- to the sweeping vistas of gods and legends and religions. The pangs of physical hunger pushed aside in the need to meet a more metaphysical hunger. Urgency is felt throughout, along with the importance and satisfaction of breathing in the present.

 In many ways, Metanoia is a journey in much the way knowing Joshua is a journey, or in much the way he travels through life. In the few years I've known him, he's taught dance in Virginia, played music in Mississippi, learned healing in Spain, and helped create a performance art space in Maine. Joshua's life, like the character in Metanoia, suggests, "I'm simply saying let's consider the opposite of everything." His open heart and brilliant, artistic mind remind us, as the book does, that "the goal isn't to unify, but to see each other."

 Joshua, and Metanoia, are inspiration. Breathe it in and let it change you.

-Naomi Buck Palagi

Preface

Metanoia (noun)
met·a·noi·a / met-*uh*-**noi**-*uh*
Metanoia, an Ancient Greek word (μετάνοια)
"A turning away from" "To change one's heart or mind"

It's not simply a decision, but a journey.
This book began long before I started writing it. Like most 20 something year olds, I was lost and stumbling through this existence while trying to make sense of it all, while trying to be who everyone was telling me I should be, while trying not to harm any more loved ones, nor be harmed by them. I began unpacking myself of the voices of my environment, so that I might find and hear my own. I gradually set down the fears, burdens, and expectations that weren't serving me, so that I could be free to live courageously and unencumbered. I even shed my birth name to mark my turning away from who I was, in hopes of becoming whoever I wanted to be. I began to repack myself with wisdoms that sparked something within me and inspired me. Joshua 1:9 had planted a seed in me, from a young age, commanding me to be strong, courageous, and fearless. So, I christened myself Joshua at the inception of my metanoia.

Many years later, during the pandemic of 2020, after flirting with the idea for a while, I decided to just start writing. I wanted to create a space where anyone seeking answers, growth, or healing could find what truths and wisdoms I had gleaned along my journey. I wanted to gently preach about the injustices of this world, not to condemn, but to help us see and make a change. I wanted to point out these cages we choose to live in, even though the keys are within our reach. I wanted to start a dialogue in which our faiths and philosophies could find peace and harmony.
I wanted to be naked and unashamed as I aimed to figure out what love is and what relationship I wanted with it.

This book has four seasons; Detachment, Endurance, Resilience, Impetus. It's a journey. Time doesn't matter. So read it linearly or pick it up from time to time and read sporadically. I hope it serves you well.

Peace and Love,

-Larry Purnell Wiley Jr.

Metanoia

The journey of changing one's heart, mind, self, or way of life.

Joshua Purnell

Flight,
....Taking
....Following Through,
....Letting
Go,

... . ………...
Metanoia; ……………….. ………………………………………………………….
…………….. ……………….. ………………………………………………………….

Being still,

eN

m

De Tach...t

*I've known rivers:
I've known rivers ancient as the world and older than the flow
of human blood in human veins.*

My soul has grown deep like the rivers.

*-Langston Hughes
The Negro Speaks of Rivers*

*E*lizabeth

      Some call it Syksy, Jesen, Autumn, Harifa, The Fall, Herbst, Harvest, there are endless names for it. Regardless, it's the same season of detachment. As trees begin to undress and birds heed the winds' whispers of change,
I sit by the river, reflecting.
The legend keepers teach us that the Titans, who came before us, forged our home around this river.

                                             and bridges
They wove roads through it, threading   under   over.
                            tunnels

 I could go on and list all the advancements that our nation has made from taming this mighty river, but those stories have already been told and continue to be told.

The legend keepers never boast of the destruction that travels with advancement.

    What purpose does history serve if not all of it is being preserved?

 Sculpting their legends, etching and erasing lines,
                                    rivers, mountains; waves and shores.

Those same Titans who carried our ancestors here and gifted us with this land stomped down forests, drove away native life, and bled black blood into our river.

          "Our river"

How can we lay claim to something so vast and infinite as this black and blue bruised river?

 These waters have been opaque for as long as I remember; still, my mind wanders here in search of clarity.

My focus breaks.

 My attention shifts down
                      to the parched copper leaves beside me;
      starting to stir,
they twirl
      as the wind ushers them along.

The sun flickers.   to see a mighty hawk mimicking their dance.
      I look up

Captivated and envious, I strain my eyes against the sun.
                                         She circles once more,
                                              then flies off
                      down the river.
"Yeah,   in the wind
    get out   to Her
        while you can"   I whisper,

A Legendkeeper once told me that some hawks can see ultraviolet rays.
Maybe the sky deepens to a rich shade of mauve when the moment is just right for migrational flight.

   I've been watching birds a lot these days.
Not intentionally, I simply keep noticing them. The natives here all fly so differently.

The seagulls,
        with their crescent shaped wings,
                              raise them higher than most.
Unless at sea,
      there they simply coast on the breeze,
          until
          diving
          in.
                they're off
      couple   and   gliding through the sky.
The crows, pound a   strong beats   strikes
        out   light   of
             quick,   the mockingbirds,
  Their style is contrasted against the   they
                                                                   seem
           The Buzzards   to be
                                                                                            at war with.
                      you don't notice them
        above.
                  until they are
            circling

   It's not their flying techniques that captivate me, but their stillness.
To have the power to challenge the clouds whenever your wingtips itched,
the ability to rise up and bathe in the setting sun on a heart's whim.

I'd never land.

I know it's all rock headed and naive,
but I would soar until my heart gave out— or my wings.
   I no longer scoff at Icarus' demise.
   I get it.
To taste freedom,
and not be expected to sink our teeth deeper and deeper
into the flesh of that fruit
again,
      and again,
           until the flesh that we bite becomes that of our very fingertips–
                         No warning could stop us.

 That's why the birds are gods of flight and we the gods of war.
They understand that not flying is part of flying as we understand that war and peace nourish each other,
so much so that they become indiscernible.

"Those moments of stillness!" I surprise myself with my own voice.
"Their wings are still… even as they soar…"

I look around and notice the torches have been lit.

I rise,
     hip stiff,
          from the unyielding roots, rebelling against the Titan built path; they are hardly noticed, blanketed under the mosaic of discarded magnolia leaves.

I wiggle my toes, assessing how conscious my feet are.

My knees sing and snap with the forgotten leaves as my soles hug the ground.

I take a step,   but continue,
    stumble,   determined
                            to walk
                                    it
                                          off.

Messipi

"Alright, I'm gonna go"
I said, slightly above a whisper but firm enough to be felt.

"Is... this it, then?"

My shoulders sank, as I turned.
"yeah, I think so" I replied, impressively softer than before. "It is."

Slightly slower than light travels, we connected;
chest to chest,
bicep to ribcage,
forearm to spine,
hand clutching shoulder blade,
flushed cheek to flooded eye.
severed heart. torn soul.

We detached.

    Our eyes met, only to again run and seek shelter,
as our levies cracked and hearts erupted.

      We had broken down each other's walls
and built a castle, by the river, with the refugee bricks.

"Look at this mess we made."

We wiped away each other's tears,
embraced,
locked eyes and smiled, for a few more seasons.

"Ok… ok… you're going to miss your flight."
said while gently applying pressure to my still bleeding cheekbone.

We locked eyes,
breathed each other in and finally…exhaled.

  I let go of a hand that I hadn't noticed grabbing
but instantly missed when I turned and walked away.

"Tell the wind to bring you back to me"

Fearing my feet would turn to stone, and my love would flood the Earth,
I didn't look back,
          as I left my home,
                    to follow the wind.

Indus

      It's difficult to describe your first flight, because there's not much to compare it to.
All we have, upon our exodus, are our prior picked expectations.
By the time we gain more experience, to contrast our genesis against, the moment is gone.
We have already chiseled those immature opinions into our memories, using those very expectations as our hammers.

      One of the Titans once swam far out to sea, farther than his brothers ever dared or dreamt.
 Legend keepers say he was in search of great riches— or was it greatness? I forget.
Regardless, the legends go on to say he lost his way while out there. When his feet finally graced the far shore, he was so excited that he gifted the natives with the name of his expected destination.

     I'm not sure what I was expecting.
 Stillness, waiting; anticipation, rustling.
Then a gentle breeze,
unnoticed,   ushering you forward,
                until your pace has already quickened
       and continues to accelerate,
     like your heart, mid sprint.
  You take a deep breath,
to compensate,   . . . g r a v i t y i s o p t i o n a l.
        and suddenly…

The Titans haven't gifted us with wings yet,
but they've crafted these massive idols to the sky gods, carved from the lightest of stone.

 No feathers,
 no wing beats,
 no stillness,
but they glide through the sky just fine.

Some hum while hovering low, as if searching for nectar.
Others shriek past, flaunting aerial acrobatics and speed.

They are works of wonder.
If only they could take flight.
                Unnoticed,
                      night approaches,
                              taking me along.

Bou Regreg

We strive to be better, smarter, faster, stronger.
We strive to be set apart, in any fashion, so that our value is not only seen, but felt.

We strive to not only be better than ourselves, but each other, our neighbors, the Titans, even the gods.
We strive to surpass them all, after suckling from their cows, then slaughtering them.

We shackle their stallions, so that they sprint at our pace.
We tame the wolves and reverence the lions, demanding the same nourishment and company for our race and pride.

Chains are where war meets peace.

It's hard to tell where that ocean starts to stop or where its sands begin to end.
There is an ebb and flow, pulling them apart while pushing them together.
It swirls them deeper into each other, keeping them indiscernible.
Intangibly coursing through our fingers, it's barely noticed or felt, especially when searched for.

Still, we compulsively and desperately sift and pine for certainty.

Legend keepers have bickered about the start of the end since the earliest dawn.
Those brothers cast their stones at the waters— and each other —marking their theories, memorializing their claims.

From up above,
it doesn't matter much.

Glancing down at the moon-stained waters,

I pray there's beach where I land.

Flight

....Taking

Metanoia

....
....
....
....
....Following..... ....
....
....
                      .

                                                           ...... Through... ... .
....being... ... .
                              ....   still..   .   .

                        ....
         .   . . Letting   go   . ...
    ....

Endurance... ....

Just like moons and like suns,
With the certainty of tides,
Just like hopes springing high,
Still I'll rise.

-Maya Angelou
Still I rise

Euphrates

There was no beach…
nor any water to be seen when my feet finally reconnected with the earth.
My heels fought against the driest, rockiest soil I had ever smelled.
I could taste the arid air, as it callously robbed the moisture from my tongue.

The legend keepers tell of a time when the gods and the Titans were at odds.
Only one man found favour in their sight.
So they burdened him with the weight of the world, as the clouds began to flood the earth.
Several cultures have documented this story; you can go read whichever one you are comfortable with.— the specifics don't matter. What matters is what came after.

    The Titans, united and swore they would never be washed away again.
They found a dry plain and began building.

They built and built, aiming their tower to pierce the heavens.

                              The gods came down.

"So, this is what they have begun.
Now, nothing they plan will be impossible.
Come! Let Us go down and confuse the people with different languages,
that they will no longer be able to understand each other."

                They shook their heads
                  and the tower
                      crumbled
                            along with
                                  their
                                        unity
                                The Titans and Earth drifted apart.

    The gods chastised the Titans as if they were toddlers…
Pulling them away from their sandcastle masterpiece, kicking, babbling, and screaming.

It's the same way we train dogs and condition slaves.

No explanation, just "No!" as they take us away from what we were doing "wrong",
                reorienting us to the "right" direction,
                    once again sending us away.

*   In that way, the gods scattered them all over the world.*

*S*harda

When elephants become separated, if left alone too long, they sink into a depression and die of a broken heart.
I wonder if the same is true for gods.

   I know it's true for The Titans.
Like an unwritten melody or half painted sunset, one titan sat alone not knowing what he lacked,
                                                                                                                                          but the void was felt.
So lonely and incomplete was he, that he laid around and slept until a companion appeared.
She brought a spark of life to him and dared him to be bold.
Together they rebelled against the gods and set out to explore the world.
The rest is history– not her story, but their story, nonetheless,
                                                                        neither the least.
What benefit do we provide for the gods?

Some legends say the gods made us because they needed companionship,
Some say they needed help tending their gardens and flocks.
Some say we are their pawns in an infinite, intricate war.
Some say we are their mirrors; what happens when we crack
                                                      and
                                                        break away?
"Shāh māt" I said,   Is that how gods are slain?
 Releasing my finger from the elephant shaped bishop.
My shoulder collided with the board, scattering the pieces.
Some things are universal and beyond language,
War and Respect are on that list.

   In a language unfamiliar to my ears, I was told to pick up the pieces.
I picked myself up instead.
I knew better, but a free spirit makes the body bold.

   During the Great War– Which? …It doesn't matter –a Titan appeared. She held us in her lap, comforting us as blood rained down in the east and clouds of fear approached from the west. She told tales of how fearful and meek she once was. She not only gave us peace and hope to believe in, but also inspired us to rebel against fear daily.

   Fire terrifies me, so I've decided to be cremated.
So does drowning, so I long to be set free by the river. I don't know which, yet.
Hopefully, the wind will get me there.

     Before I could finish rising, I was back on the ground, eye level to the helpless king. I flattened my hand against the cold floor, still striving to rise. Footsteps approached, vibrating against my cheek, continuing until they greeted my hand with a firm embrace. I winced, too stubborn to acknowledge it.
     I looked up to see a hand caressing the handle of a dagger, it was either rusted or recently used— the setting sun wasn't cooperating; She too was against me. Realizing that fire against fire was getting me nowhere, I grabbed the king with my free hand and began to reset the battlefield.

   My queen was taken before the game started; boldly, I pushed her pawn forward two spaces, leaving it bloodstained.
"The only idols I cling to are those I can afford to lose."

Mekong

It ended in a stalemate, as with most stalemates, neither side was happy about it. Before leaving, the general placed a bowl on top of the barren board. My stomach growled as I skeptically looked inside. After sniffing it— as if my nose could sense hidden danger —I began pawing at it.

One of my teachers once said,
"When we have more food than we need, then the gods have no power over us"

Some Legends say that in the beginning, we were surrounded by plants and trees yielding the most delicious of fruits, but what were we expected to do once The Fall came? Stand by as the leaves fell, and days grew colder and shorter? We dressed ourselves in those copper leaves and sought shelter.

Other keepers tell of a young Titan, who was gifted a mighty hatchet.
He tested its merit against a tree known for yielding bitter-sweet fruit.
When confronted by a towering voice in the garden, he confessed and was shown mercy because of his honesty.

They go on to say that he grew into a great warrior and noble leader, who led his brothers to freedom.
No one mentions his garden.
A garden so prodigious that he used 246 hands to tend it— or 123, depending on the math.

When disharmony strikes homes, elders speak of duty to their youth.
When chaos engulfs nations, citizens cry out for great leaders.

We only call on prophets in times of famine.
We only praise gods in times of abundance.

We love the sun until the fields grow torrid.
We curse the rain until the rivers run dry.

We crave knowledge until it teaches us death.
We worship time at the sacrifice of existence.

A flipped coin is more likely to land on the side it started on.
The same can't be said for tables.

The more I paced,
The smaller the room seemed.

The more I thought,
The more crowded my mind became.

The more I tried to stay calm,
the smaller my patience grew.

Finally anger trumped peace.

The pieces fell to the ground— I didn't mourn the fallen soldiers —and the empty bowl rang, as it spun, singing to my hosts that I was rioting.

I didn't care. I hoped they answered.

Still circling the room, I grabbed the severed table leg and cracked it against the door like a mighty whip.

I scanned my cage for possible moves, rationing away the poor choices,
and then there were none.

There was no one.

I sat.

Alone.

My heart and lungs continued raging, but I gave up.

I looked over to the window, again, considering insanity.

The sun had left me.
The moon snuggled into a blanket of clouds atop a mountain.

I'd never taken one in with my own eyes, but the Legendkeepers spoke of them often.
So many stories of transformative moments.

I longed for a metanoia of my own.

I would forsake all destinations in life and go climb that mountain; nothing, not even the gods themselves could stop me.

As I laid on the floor, the air reminded me that I should be cold.

The season of detachment had passed.

Now was the time to endure.

*S*tyx*

I awoke to three familiar legs. One brutishly caressed my back, while the other two stood by.

"Again"

I was instructed to reset the chess board.
Squinting in the light, as my eyes became reacquainted with the well-rested sun, I looked over at the other three-legged elephant in the room.

I smirked at my small victory and raised a question, with my shoulders.
My host glared, pulled up a chair, directly in front of me, and sat.
I assembled the board, on my bed, and went to grab a chair.

    As I walked away, I was advised otherwise.
Not all the words made it across the language barrier, but the tone and flying limb were great context clues.
I sat, awaiting white's move,
                      once again queen-less.

Why would the gods take away the Titans' castle?
 I've been thinking about this a lot, recently.— I've had the free time —The keepers didn't leave much detail in any of their accounts.
What was so wrong about building a tower to reach the—

"Oh! They were looking up… instead of within!"

My startled opponent raised an eyebrow.
Shaking my head, to defuse, I castled, (King's side.)

Another Stalemate.
Then stalemate.
  then another.
     then another.
        The sun left again, but our kings still refused to fall.

A suspended torch imitates my resting friend.
My stomach roars with annoyance and impatience.
It's ignored.
My pawn crosses over.
"Queen." I demand, accomplishedly.
It's ignored.
I slowly reach.
It's ignored.

I return her to the field.

She's taken.
It's ignored

Another stalemate.

Then another.

 The sun sets
   Stalemate.
   Stalemate
     then another.
       my pawn promotes.
        Its ignored
Night rises.
        another stalemate
          Then another.
Sun returns
         then another
           Pawn promotes.
            Its ignored
             Pawn Promotes.
           Its ignored
Night approaches.
another stalemate.
     pawn pawn
     Its ignored.
Then another
Queen.
Pawn promotes
Elephants collide.
Stalemate.

Then another.

pawn
pawn.
     Titian lunges forward.

Pawn races ahead.
       Stallion veers to the right.

   Pawn steps forward.
 Stallion sprints.

Night approaches.
    Elephant swings.

Night pinned.
Titan leaves the garden.

Dragon rises.
Titan keeps walking forward.

Bishop.
Elephant.

Castle (Queen's side).
Castle (Queen's side).

Titian.
Pawns headbutt.

Stallion sprints.
Night charges.

Elephant defends.
Titian.

We built a castle by the river.
Prophets throw stones.

Titian climbs.
Prophets cast rocks.
Its ignored.

Titian climbs.
Night falls.

Titan faces god, boldly, stealing fire.
The tower falls.

"Checkmate"

My stomach roars
It's ignored.

I sit.

The sun sets.
It's ignored

I sit.

The bowl rings
It's ignored

The moon kisses the mountain, outside the window.

I dream.

Clarity and Lunacy dance.

 I wake up.

I reach out my hand, and take the key,
leaving the general lifeless, while clutching the queen.

Freedom sings as I fumble over the possibilities.
I don't look back.

I hatch as the sun begins to do the same.

 Lost and liberated, I turn my feet to face the mountain off in the distance and continue my flight.

C

An

Li e

i

S

Re

I'm so darn glad He let me try it again
'Cause my last time on earth, I lived a whole world of sin
I'm so glad that I know more than I knew then
Gonna keep on tryin'
'Til I reach my highest ground

-Stevie Wonder
Higher Ground

Tizon

I had lost all sense of time.
I assumed the shackle on my wrist functioned just fine,
but there was no reason to check it.
The god of time had no power over me, here.

Despite being lost, my feet continued forward confidently.
Was this the brink of insanity?
Racing boldly towards something with no guarantee.
Believing in something despite there being no evidence.

Some of the elders call that faith,
Yet, most warn that intangible faith is unwise.

I wonder which of their gods will win,
The one they love or the one they fear.

My feet paused
           at a cliff.

      Even the pale amber vegetation
                           stopped and held its
                                                   breath
                                                   before
Beyond, the earth was bloodstained crimson,   tip-
                                                         toeing
                    as   off the ledge.

                   the sun

                  soothingly,

               relaxed

                 Her legs

                 into

                the
        across   mountain
Looking   river,   still beckoned me forward.

             resting below.

Its base was a deep soot— evidence of being burned by the jagged fiery streaks carved up its side —while rivers of snow trickled down from the clouds.
I take a step, stumble, but continue, determined to walk
                                           it
                                         off.

Have you ever gotten lost while climbing a mountain?
You'd think it would be easy to just go up, right?

Not all the ways up
               get you up
                           to the "up" that you were aiming for,
                                             from the ground.

I expected the wilderness to be where I struggled.
I was prepared to endure the standard 40 days and 40 nights,
but I cleared it in… no time.

The mountain required a bit more mustering to clear.

At the summit, I realized that the one beckoning me was much farther away.
I took in the scenery a moment, scanning for any overlooked beauty,
then climbed back down
                     into the wilderness,
                               my feet once again facing the mountain.

One of my teachers once said
"A thorn of experience is worth a wilderness of warning"

Perhaps the gods only meant to warn us, in the same manner that a parent warns that fire is hot,
not because fire is innately evil, but because it must be handled carefully.
One spark creates light and warmth, yet has the potential to destroy an entire garden.

Sometimes, I imagine the god of Genesis as a young father, learning as He goes, warning His son with His hands tied, that if he is not careful, he will fall.
I can't imagine the heartbreak and hard learned lessons that father was scarred with, when His only begotten son was condemned to wander away from him.

Perhaps the gods have been learning alongside us,
in the same manner that teachers learn while sculpting students.

Perhaps parents learn while pruning and watering each child
and healers learn while waging wars on internal battle fields.

Some legend keepers speak of a war waged in paradise.

Perhaps the cancerous separation of sin was first taught to the gods by that fallen star.
The bringer of light, who first burned them.
Then again by man
 then again by man
  then again by man, until the earth was on fire with sin and the gods had no choice but to flood it and start anew.

Still, it survives, continuing to burn, within us.

Impetus

*Sometimes a crumb falls
From the tables of joy,
Sometimes a bone
Is flung.*

*To some people
Love is given,
To others
Only heaven.*

*- Langston Hughes
Luck*

In the beginning...

Heavens... Earth

Darkness... let there be Light

Day.... Night.
It was good.

Land... Sea.
It was good.

Creeping vegetation... Fruiting trees.
It was good

Sun... Moon.
It was good.

Fish... Birds.
It was good.

Wild animals... Livestock
It was good.

Man... Woman.

"Something is off."   *Tree of life... Tree of knowledge of good and evil.*

The trees aren't balanced.

Tree of life. Tree of Knowledge...of good and evil.

Tree of life. Tree of Knowledge ~~of good and evil.~~

"Hmmm…no. The legends say we already had knowledge, so that wouldn't entice us."
 "Be fruitful and multiply, and fill the earth and subdue it; and have dominion over the fish of the sea and over the birds of the air and over every living thing that moves upon the earth"

Surly we couldn't reign over animals without knowledge.
Tree of life… Tree of Death?
"*When you eat from it you will certainly die.*"

Tree of Life… Tree of Creation?
Perhaps to create or be a creator, we need to know what good is.
"*It was good*"

Tree of life. Tree of Knowledge ~~of good and evil.~~
Tree of life. Tree of Knowledge... of making good and demolishing bad

How else would we know if the creation was sufficient or even necessary?
How else would we know if our works were complete and good,
or flawed and needing to be broken and reset for repair?

Why didn't the gods want this for us?
Why have the tree there if we shouldn't eat from it?

Perhaps the gods really did make us in their image, weaknesses and all.
Made in their image, we omnipotently have free will.
                                                                           They couldn't stop us.
                        They could only warn us.

They warned us with death, to deter us, but the moon showed us the flawed logic.
It showed us that we have the power to choose and manifest our own path.

Respecting our free will, the gods stood by and watched in suspense.

The moment we gave into our will and chose to bite that fruit,
we immediately began manifesting our own realities.
Seeing we were naked and cunning, we crafted clothing for ourselves from leaves.
When we heard the gods walking in the garden, in the cool of the day, we hid.

Then The Lord called out to Adam and said to him 'where are you?"

High off sin, and irrational, we came out of hiding and explained our reason.

"Who told you were naked? Have you eaten of the fruit?

What did we choose when we ate from that other tree? Rejection of paradise;
death, infinite suffering, and cancerous separation?

Could the Tree of Life simply be access to paradise;
immortality, everlasting life, and communion with the gods?

Could the two trees be one?
"The tree of life was also in the midst of the garden and was the tree of knowledge of good and evil."

Some legends say that Heaven was once very near to the earth,
so near that one could stretch up one's hand from the garden and touch it.

Upon our eviction, the gods generously replaced our fig leaves with animal skins, before
sending us out to encounter death.
  "Man has now become like one of us, ~~knowing good and evil.~~
                                      —knowing how to create and reason—
*They must not be allowed to reach out their hand and take also from the tree of life
and eat and live forever."
So, the Lord God banished them from the Garden...*

"So this is what we walked into; this is what we left paradise for?"
I thought out loud, as I gazed over the horizon.
Some bittersweet fruit and the ability to manifest our lives.
but what makes sin so innate within us, now?
What causes this consistent choice of cancerous separation? An alternative directive.

Some Legends blame the moon for our exile, yet also honor her as a co-creator of us.
They say she saw us eat the forbidden fruit then told what she saw.
Many blame Lucifer,
Others blame Eve or Pandora.
Ultimately, it's the same choice of separation,
 quickly followed by emotions; shame and fear as we hide.
Anger and judgment rise as we blame and kill our siblings.
More fear follows as we imagine the consequences of our actions and the impending punishment from the gods.

If we were made in their image, we omnipotently have free will.
Why do we cling to sin as an Achilles?— as if it has made us lame in this walk of life and we have no choice but to stumble through it.

 If we are taught to believe that we can move mountains and that God is omnipotent— which by deductive reasoning makes us all powerful— why are we still held captive by sin?
What is sin?
Was sin the action of eating the fruit or the fruit itself?

I wonder if the gods have eaten of the fruit or if we were its taste testers.
Why did they plant it?
Did they really plant the tree or is it a metaphor for something?

 Everything is a metaphor, right?
What does the fruit mean?
What kind of fruit did the tree bare?
What if its love?
Could it be so simple?
As with most things, in life, the only way to truly appreciate something is to exist without it for a season.

When we pray for courage, we are given moments to be courageous.
With strength, we build it by overcoming heavy loads.
With patience, we are presented opportunities to exercise patience.
When striving for wisdom, our eyes are opened to opportunities to make wise choices.
What happens when we choose love?

As with all the other growing pains of life,
perhaps the only way to fully understand and appreciate love,
is to endure the trauma of separation from it, while limping through life without it.
Perhaps the more profound your wound, the deeper your capacity to understand and give love.

Is that why the gods warned us not to bite the forbidden fruit?
To have Life, connection, and joy, there must be Death, detachment, and pain.

To this day it's the same bittersweet fruit that entices yet terrifies us.

Love.

The Greeks taught me 7 love stories.

"Would you like to dance?"

"I'd love to"   *Eros*

We connected.
        Chest to chest,
                bicep to ribcage,
                        forearm to spine, hand cradling shoulder blade,

        heartbeat to breath.

                We kissed.

        Some things are compulsory and absent of logic,
        a strong impulse that you can't silence or ignore,
        a burning desire that consumes your rationality.

The more you fight it, the stronger it becomes.
            Eventually you have to say it out loud,
Whether to yourself or someone else
        you must let it out.

                "what if…"

That's all it takes to spark the flame, and once it catches fire, there is no stopping it.

*L*udus

"I have to ask you something.
 But first, you must promise me, no matter what, promise me,
                                                                you won't get up."

" I PROMISE"

"Look up"
I paused as we lay there gazing at the star speckled ceiling.
We had rediscovered our youth and its joy as the sky was falling.
What a time to be alive.

            "What if we could touch it?"

Before the fruit was bitten, we were but mere children in the garden.
Or more so, we were puppies,
                    not knowing the power of our bite and curiosity,
                        innocently nipping at everything that caught our eye,
                                    pure hearted curiosity and wonder.

Perhaps the gods' warning wasn't to save us, but an effort to protect the rest of the world from the impending destruction of our freewill. After we bit, the gods had no choice but to send us outside.

*They must not be allowed to reach out their hand and take also from the tree of life
and eat and live forever."*

So, the Lord God banished them from the Garden...

            The promise was broken early that morning.

"Hey, can I bum a smoke off you?"
"Sure"

"Got a lighter?"

"Heh. Nice try"
        "Get outta here".
                He said,
                      "Let there be light"

They leave out the part about the sky particles colliding
 as thunder boomed and fire rushed to kiss the ground
 piercing through the endless ocean, shooting the sea up to the heavens,
  as if offering the Titans a drink for all their effort.

The mist seemed infinite and never landing as it hovered over the scorched, moist earth.

It is there that Prometheus landed and the story of his road to redemption begins.

The muddy earth baked and solidified.
The hovering mist breathed itself into the godlike man.

Los dios habían dado a luz
The gods had given birth
                and planted Lucifer in the earth.
It is out of him, bone of his bone flesh of his flesh,
that life emerged and we– gods and humans alike –began to know company and sculpt.

They walked in the mist of the gods enjoying the fruits of their labor.

Except for that one tree. The one the gods had forbidden.

I wonder if Adam and Eve knew that this was their heavenly do-over,
 their clean slate, and redemption back into paradise.

Abba, trying to play fair, still gently warned them.
"You may eat of any tree in the garden except that fig tree"

What if I told you that the type of tree isn't important?
Perhaps the gods picked a placebo tree.
It was the heart of our actions that caused us to fall.

Like Lucifer,
        we have had free will since the dawn of time.

Like Prometheus' decent with knowledge, or Zeus' rebellion,
                                  biting the fruit
        was our first time playing with fire, and just like our forefathers,

                we once again burned the gods and broke away.

I look up to see two great black birds with huge wings circling in the sun.
Buzzards.
I can tell by the way the tips of their wings angle up.

Two legend keeps once disagreed about the story of these great birds.
Some consider them omens of death.
"Am I dying? Can they sense hunger consuming me from within?
Maybe this was a mistake; at least back there I had food."
My stomach roars.
It's ignored.

Looking ahead, the mountain seems just as far away as it was from the tower window.
Still outside the jurisdiction of the gods of time, I don't know how long I've been wandering in this wilderness.
My stomach roars.
I continue to ignore it as my feet drag my body forward.

"What else did they say about those birds?"
They bathe in sunlight every morning, allowing the ultraviolet rays to cleanse them.
Other legends view them as creator gods, and symbols of cycles and rebirth.

I decide to head toward them for a closer look as they glide off towards a mountain.
My pace quickens with excitement.
My heart hadn't roared this fiercely since the penultimate battle back at the tower.

Cold wars never end, they simply fade into the background and become microaggressions,
building pressure until the levies break, releasing all the residual damage and tension from the first battle.

I look up as trees begin to shelter me from the sun.
The branches thicken, making the vultures hard to see.
I lose them but continue up.

The gods of time catch up with me as the air grows colder.
My body cries out, from the torn calloused sole of my right foot and through both of my burning calves.
My knees are fine, numb,
                but my thighs feel every step as my stomach crawls along,
                                                  dragging us with it.
I make it through the wilderness,
as the sun bleeds a bronze scarlet all over the sky
Night was beginning to climb up, bracing herself, using clouds as foot holds.
I mimic her as I scale the last stretch of mountain, too steep to walk.

I know better than to look too far up, and definitely not down— I look anyway.
My right-hand slips, and my heart drops to the ground, almost pulling me with it.
I take a breath.
        breath
          breath
    Then another, reeling my heart back in.
            Once composed, I continue up.

Philia

I wonder how high up The Titans were when the gods demolished the tower?

They say there was once a great general who came quite close to conquering the world.

There came a point when his valiant army grew weary and homesick.
Despite all the new adventures and glory of victory, they missed their old lives.
Some started to mutiny.
The king squashed their attempts but grew increasingly paranoid and lost his closest friends.

Eventually he died. Of what? Legend keepers aren't quite sure.

A broken heart?
Malaria?
Poison?

I guess, what I'm getting at is that maybe we give these gods too much credit— or too little.
I'm simply saying let's consider the opposite of everything.

What if the gods didn't collapse the tower?
Maybe it was an inside job.

Before we began farming, settling, and sheltering ourselves from the uncertainty of nature, we roamed, traveled, and explored.

The world was our home, not just our pueblos.
Maybe some citizens, building the tower, missed the old days.
Maybe one of those forefathers looked up and thought,

  "This isn't the way".

Maybe he was terrified to speak against the masses, his brothers, for he knew their anger would consume him.
Maybe, speaking out was the only way.

One morning, he woke up, before building time, climbed the tower and shouted down to them.
He told them they were looking in the wrong direction.
He told them that the gods were within him… and all of them.
As expected, they became enraged and started collecting stones to throw at him.

He didn't stop preaching
"The only way to reach the gods is to look within!"

Rocks began to soar
"Not up!"

They kept throwing
"Not up!"

He kept preaching
"Not up…"

Hearts were turned.

Those who believed in him began throwing tower supplies at his attackers.

Both sides continued casting stones.

Both sides tore into the tower for ammunition.

Each stone thrower fought their personal battles and internal wars that day.

They shook their heads,
 destroying the tower, ultimately reorienting us back to our original objective;
confused and concussed we scattered across the earth to *"be fruitful and multiply"*

Our tower was a fruitless effort and waste of time and resources…
our forefathers could never reach "the heavens" that way.

Perhaps at the tower, we were too unified.   The goal isn't to unify, but to see each other,
Perhaps in the garden, we were too unified   to really see each other.
Perhaps in heaven, we were too unified.   When we truly see each other,
Perhaps on Mt. Olympus we were too unified.   we see ourselves.

We become so engrossed in building our towers to reach the gods we idolize that we stop seeing the heavens within us and each other.
Mindlessly grabbing at stones or heartlessly throwing them,
We don't realize that we're all part of the same divine
                                                        kinship.
              To simply gaze into the eyes of another soul transcends us.

I'd bet 30 pieces of silver that Cain didn't look Able in the eyes when he killed him.
If he had looked into his brother's eyes that day, there's no way he could have pulled the trigger.

I used the last of my strength to pull myself up over the ledge and collapsed. Looking up my eyes followed the buzzards as they did a final lap around, then roosted in a tree.
My eyes traced its branches back to its trunk, then its trunk down into the earth.

There, my eyes met another pair in the silver moon light; sad, lost, and exhausted, Her eyes were just like mine.

*S*torge

"Abba!"

"Abba?"

"ABBA!?"

I was so busy yelling that I didn't notice… until,

A tremendous, mighty, windstorm tore at the mountain.

After the wind, there came earthquaking thunder.

After the earthquake came fiery lightning.

After the fire, a gentle whisper….

"Why are you here?"

I woke to the warmth of the sun, closer than I'd ever felt before.
The golden blossoms of the tree seemed to be ablaze.
They were.

Below it,
        unphased by the flames, She ate.

Compelled by curiosity— and famine —I stepped forward.
                              My stomach roared.
                                    She ignored it.
I proceeded with caution and respect.

She didn't look up until I was an arm length away.

Within reach was a white wafer, similar to the one She was pecking at.

        I knelt down, and slowly grabbed it.

I brought it to my face, sniffing it, as my mouth watered; it reminded me of coriander.

I broke it and ate.

It was good.
Sweet, but not too sweet.

I devoured it and moved closer for more.

They were scattered all over, beneath the shade of the tree,
                                             I ate,
I'd forgotten.   ate   and I ate.
                                                    and I ate,
I looked up.   and ate,
                                                I ate and I ate
We locked eyes again, then both returned to eating.

"Why are you here?"

I still had no answer for myself.

The legend keepers preach about a shepherd who wandered far from home to fulfill a promise he made to his father. He led his father's sheep on a journey that took far longer than anticipated.
 They got lost in a wilderness much like this one.

He, like many other heroes, found enlightenment, courage, and death atop a mountain.
Why do so many legends set these divine-mortal interactions atop mountains?

Does it paint a better story?
Is the climb up a testament to the protagonist's efforts?
Or is it that ascending these mountains feels as impossible as reaching the gods?

Atop the mountain, in the wilderness, the shepherd's father gave him instructions to pass on to his sheep.

They didn't listen.
            Back home, in my village, men refuse to follow directions.

A water goddess once joked, "If the instructions had been written down, in the garden, it would have been a man that bit the fruit… not a woman."

The legend keeps say that when the creator gods came down to sculpt the earth, the male gods disrespected the goddess of love and sweet water. They felt they didn't need her.

She became offended and went to the moon, taking her sweet water with her.

The rivers ran dry,   cracked as it cried out in thirst.
            vegetation died,   and
                        the earth became barren

The other gods struggled to fulfill their tasks. Confused and frustrated they went to complain to God.

He did a quick count, and in typical godlike fashion asked questions to which He already knew the answer.

"How many of you did I send?"

"17", replied the chorus.

"How many of you are here?"

"16" they sang in disharmony.

"Where is Oshun?"

God went to the moon.

"Oshun, Why are you here?"

She vents to God, then returns to Earth.

The others apologize for taking her for granted.

She forgives them, but warns,

"Don't let it happen again"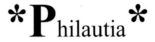

Water returned to the earth.

I heard and smelled it before I saw it.
I stepped forward to welcome it.
I leaned my head back.
Standing… with my mouth open wide
Just as my preschool teacher had taught me.

Rain.

The sweetest I had ever tasted. I gave thanks and drank.

Full-bellied and soaked, I scanned around for shelter.

To my left there was a cave.

I grabbed a few wafers from under the golden blossomed tree for later and walked toward the cave.

I stopped.

Where did She go?

I continued to the cave.

Agape

Not so long ago,
        in the southeast,
                during a Tsunami, a baby hippo was orphaned.
After the storm she found herself alone and scared all the way in Africa.
There she met an elderly tortoise.
She clung to his side, just as she had with her mother.
He adopted her.
        They had no obligation to love each other… no biological ties,
                              nor social expectations.

                Love is a gift.
        True gifts are given without any expectation or debt.

*T*etelestai*

I stepped out as the sun was lying down.
The smell of rain lingered in the air as I approached the edge.

Finally, that once distant mountain now stood beneath me.
As I looked out across the horizon, I saw the footsteps of my long journey.
Each landmark a bookmark in the pages of my past seasons.
I'm not the same soul I was by the river, nor at the tower, nor in the wilderness.

                                their reach.
                    beyond   stared up at me.
                  just   Grey clouds
          my toes
            raised
The palms of the earth
I knew there was sweet water below,
though I couldn't see it, I could hear Her calling.

The wind gently nudged me,
                "Get on with it"

I breathed Him in,   weightless,
          slightly more

                                            leapt in
                                  and   to
I took a deep breath, got a running start, spread my wings,   the sun.

Tetelestai.

Epilogue

Metanoia

I started this journey, in the garden, by the river.
When we submit to the wind, we don't know where its currents will take us.
We forfeit our will, plans, and ego.
There are moments we must be patient and flexible, while we wait for the next warm air current.
There are times of storms where we must be still and endure until the skies clear.
There are seasons we must detach from beliefs, loved ones, and thoughts no longer serving us.

The tower not only taught me endurance, but its solitude gave me time and space to look within and face those unresolved cold wars.

The wilderness re-sparked and fortified my will. Each step and roar of my stomach, posed the question,
"Are you sure?" I wasn't.
Still, I kept going.

Atop the mountain— all of them —I met God; but, like flying, it wasn't what I expected.
The first time She spoke, I was too busy yelling to hear Her.

"Why are you here?"

Why was I chasing mountains to find something that lived and breathed within me?
Look around. You've been to the mountain. Go down. Teach and spread agape, UNCONDITIONAL LOVE.

I chose to believe that Abba…the gods…the universe…love has me and works in my favour.
It has never left me to fall. That faith makes leaping almost effortless.

A letter from the Author

To my dear Castle,

There will come a day when I'm not around.
I want you to know that I believe in you.
I want you to know that you are deeply loved, unconditionally.
I want you to know that you are not obliged to anything that doesn't vibrate in harmony with your soul.
I want you to know that nothing could ever cause this mountain of pride that I have for you to waver.
However, much more importantly, please continue to strive to be proud of you.
Let the voice of your heart and conscience be your council, not my voice nor anyone else's.

I've been collecting and chiseling my own commandments to live by.
Perhaps they will serve you well:

Follow Through.

Spread Agape.

Honour your anger.

Strive for stillness.

Find balance and structure; you are a mountain.

Accept anything offered in pure kindness.

Start where you are. Use what you have. Do what you can.

Be kind to yourself; it will help you be kind to others.

Be flexible and let things go.

Be a conduit: Focus and Direction; Observation and Submission

Be strong and of good courage. Do not be afraid nor be dismayed, for I am with you, wherever you go.

with love,

Abba

Made in the USA
Middletown, DE
02 September 2024